# Quick CSS Authoring

I0014479

Published By

Sandeep Kumar Patel.

# Table of Contents

Contents

# Chapter 1 Introduction to SASS

SASS is also called as "Sassy CSS" and it stands for Syntactically Awesome Style Sheet. It is used for Authoring CSS. It provides an awesome programmatic platform to a CSS developer for authoring. To know more about SASS use follows this link http://sass-lang.com/about.html .

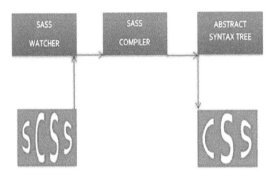

## Objective

In this Chapter, "We will learn Sass Installation in windows, configuring SCSS Watcher and creating a sample SCSS Rule file ".

## Going Ahead

We need RUBY installed in our system to install SASS. To check ruby installation in your machine issue ruby with option -v. It will print the installed ruby version for your machine. Below screen shows this step.

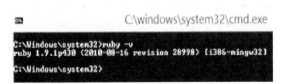

You can download and install ruby from http://rubyinstaller.org/downloads/. SASS is an RUBY based package (Gem) Issue gem command with install and sass as parameters. The below screen shows installation of SASS gem.

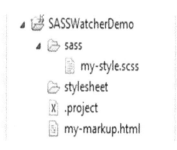

```
C:\windows\system32\c

C:\Windows\system32>gem install sass
Successfully installed sass-3.2.10
1 gem installed
Installing ri documentation for sass-3.2.10...
Updating class cache with 406 classes...
Installing RDoc documentation for sass-3.2.10...

C:\Windows\system32>_
```

Let's create a basic java script project with two directory **sass, stylesheet** in our eclipse editor. Let's create **my-style.scss** file to write all our sass based style rules. Also create a html file called **my-markup.html** for writing the HTML markups. Below screen shows the project structure.

- SASSWatcherDemo
  - sass
    - my-style.scss
  - stylesheet
  - .project
  - my-markup.html

To run SASS Watcher issue the sass command with **--watch** option followed by source and target separated by colon. The watcher observes that there is a file called **my-style.scss** inside the sass file and immediately creates a corresponding css file called **my-style.css** inside the **stylesheet** directory. Watcher is responsible for maintaining sync between these two directories. Below screen shows the command to start the SASS watcher.

```
C:\Windows\System32\cmd.exe - sass  --watch sass:stylesh

F:\html-workspace\SASSWatcherDemo>ls
my-markup.html  sass   stylesheet

F:\html-workspace\SASSWatcherDemo>sass --watch sass:stylesheet
>>> Sass is watching for changes. Press Ctrl-C to stop.
    overwrite stylesheet/my-style.css
```

In my-markup.html we have our HTML code which has a student details table. Also you can see the header part is calling **my-style.css** file. The code inside is as below.

```
<!DOCTYPE html>
<html>
<head>
  <title>TS : SASS Watcher Demo</title>
```

```html
    <link rel='stylesheet' type="text/css" href='./stylesheet/my-style.css'>
</head>
<body>
  <table class='ts-student-table'>
    <thead>
      <tr>
        <th>NAME</th>
        <th>ROLL</th>
        <th>MARK</th>
        <th>COUNTRY</th>
      </tr>
    </thead>
    <tbody>
      <tr class='odd'>
        <td>Sandeep</td>
        <td>001</td>
        <td>235</td>
        <td>India</td>
      </tr>
      <tr class='even'>
        <td>John</td>
        <td>002</td>
        <td>335</td>
        <td>US</td>
      </tr>
      <tr class='odd'>
        <td>Stephen</td>
        <td>003</td>
        <td>135</td>
        <td>UK</td>
      </tr>
      <tr class='even'>
        <td>Philip</td>
        <td>004</td>
        <td>139</td>
        <td>Germany</td>
      </tr>
```

```
    </tbody>
  </table>
</body>
</html>
```

This **my-style.scss** file contains the sass code rule for our markup. You can see it is written in a different syntax and a structured way. The code inside this SCSS file is as below.

```
table.ts-student-table{
  border-spacing:0;
  border-collapse:collapse;
  thead{
   background:#000;
   color:#fff;
  }
  tbody{
   tr.even{
    background:#cccccc;
   }
   tr.odd{
    background:#808080;
   }
  }
 }
```

While writing these codes inside **my-style.scss** file the sass watcher observes the changes and pick it up calls the sass compiler. The sass compiler then converts the sass code to abstract syntax tree object notation. From this notation it can be converted to css code inside **my-style.css**. You can observer the command prompt of the watcher below.

```
C:\Windows\System32\cmd.exe - sass --watch sass:styleshe...

F:\html-workspace\SASSWatcherDemo>sass --watch sass:stylesheet
>>> Sass is watching for changes. Press Ctrl-C to stop.
    overwrite stylesheet/my-style.css
>>> Change detected to: F:/html-workspace/SASSWatcherDemo/sass/my-style.scss
    overwrite stylesheet/my-style.css
>>> Change detected to: F:/html-workspace/SASSWatcherDemo/sass/my-style.scss
    overwrite stylesheet/my-style.css
>>> Change detected to: F:/html-workspace/SASSWatcherDemo/sass/my-style.scss
    overwrite stylesheet/my-style.css
>>> Change detected to: F:/html-workspace/SASSWatcherDemo/sass/my-style.scss
    overwrite stylesheet/my-style.css
>>> Change detected to: F:/html-workspace/SASSWatcherDemo/sass/my-style.scss
    overwrite stylesheet/my-style.css
>>> Change detected to: F:/html-workspace/SASSWatcherDemo/sass/my-style.scss
    overwrite stylesheet/my-style.css
>>> Change detected to: F:/html-workspace/SASSWatcherDemo/sass/my-style.scss
    overwrite stylesheet/my-style.css
>>> Change detected to: F:/html-workspace/SASSWatcherDemo/sass/my-style.scss
    overwrite stylesheet/my-style.css
```

Finally the css gets applied to our student table markup and output looks like below screen.

file:///F:/html-workspace/SASSWatcherDemo/my-markup.html

| NAME | ROLL | MARK | COUNTRY |
|------|------|------|---------|
| Sandeep | 001 | 235 | India |
| John | 002 | 335 | US |
| Stephen | 003 | 135 | UK |
| Philip | 004 | 139 | Germany |

# Chapter 2 SASS Interactive Shell

SASS provides an Interactive Shell prompt for use to test scripts. You can see my previous post to get started with SASS. Sass Interactive shell can be called using **SASS -i** command in prompt. A successful call will show you sass prompt.

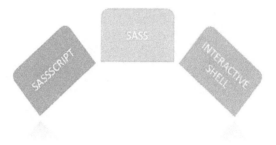

### Objective

In this Chapter, "We will see how to open a SASS Interactive Shell and some use with arithmetic operations on pixel and Hex colors".

### Going Ahead

Check the below screenshot for calling SASS interactive shell on command prompt.

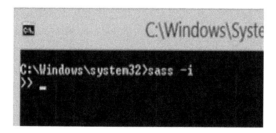

SASS interactive shell can be used for arithmetic operation on Pixel values. Like 10px + 20px = 30px.Check the below screenshot for other example,

```
C:\Windows\system32>sass -i
>> 10px + 20px
30px
>> 30px - 5px
25px
>> 25px * 2
50px
>> 50px / 2
25px
>>
```

SASS interactive shell is also capable of Hexadecimal color code arithmetic. Check the below screenshot for hexadecimal color code arithmetic.

```
C:\Windows\system32>sass -i
>> #CCC000 + #808080
#ffff80
>> #FFFFFF - #C0C0C0
#3f3f3f
>>
```

# Chapter 3 Understanding SASS Features

SASS (Syntactically Awesome Style Sheet) is a CSS authoring framework. You can see previous chapter for basic explanation and installation of SASS. There are many features offered by SASS framework.

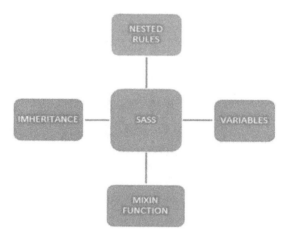

## Objective

In this Chapter, "We will understand Nesting, Variables, Mixin, Inheritance, Placeholder, SASS Script implementation".

## Going Ahead

The HTML markup that we have used for styling is in **my-markup.html** file. This file has a HTML Table DOM with student details rows. The code is shown below.

```
<!DOCTYPE html>
<html>
<head>
  <title>TS : SASS Feature Demo</title>
  <link rel='stylesheet' type="text/css" href='./stylesheets/my-style.css'>
</head>
<body>
<table class='ts-student-table'>
  <thead>
```

```html
<tr>
  <th>NAME</th>
  <th>ROLL</th>
  <th>MARK</th>
  <th>COUNTRY</th>
</tr>
</thead>
<tbody>
<tr class='odd'>
  <td>Sandeep</td>
  <td>001</td>
  <td>235</td>
  <td>India</td>
</tr>
<tr class='even'>
  <td>John</td>
  <td>002</td>
  <td>335</td>
  <td>US</td>
</tr>
<tr class='odd'>
  <td>Stephen</td>
  <td>003</td>
  <td>135</td>
  <td>UK</td>
</tr>
<tr class='even'>
  <td>Philip</td>
  <td>004</td>
  <td>139</td>
  <td>Germany</td>
</tr>
<tr class='odd'>
  <td>Sandeep</td>
  <td>001</td>
  <td>235</td>
  <td>India</td>
```

```
      </tr>
      <tr class='even'>
        <td>John</td>
        <td>002</td>
        <td>335</td>
        <td>US</td>
      </tr>
      <tr class='odd'>
        <td>Stephen</td>
        <td>003</td>
        <td>135</td>
        <td>UK</td>
      </tr>
      <tr class='even'>
        <td>Philip</td>
        <td>004</td>
        <td>139</td>
        <td>Germany</td>
      </tr>
      <tr class='odd'>
        <td>Sandeep</td>
        <td>001</td>
        <td>235</td>
        <td>India</td>
      </tr>
      <tr class='even'>
        <td>John</td>
        <td>002</td>
        <td>335</td>
        <td>US</td>
      </tr>
      <tr class='odd'>
        <td>Stephen</td>
        <td>003</td>
        <td>135</td>
        <td>UK</td>
      </tr>
```

```
  <tr class='even'>
    <td>Philip</td>
    <td>004</td>
    <td>139</td>
    <td>Germany</td>
  </tr>
  </tbody>
</table>
</body>
</html>
```

## Nesting

This feature is very useful for authoring css. As we know SPECIFICITY while styling HTML elements takes more precedence. The generic thumb rule for css 'More Generic the Specificity more it takes the Precedence'. As we know while authoring css we face lot of situation where we need to override some css classes for many times and as development goes long ways we face situation where lot of redundant css code in our code-base. This makes the developer's life hell. SASS makes it simpler through nesting. Below code is a simple example (.SCSS) for applying style using nested rule.

```
table{
  /*style for table level*/
  thead{
    /*style for thead*/
    tr{
      /*style for tr*/
      th{
        /*style for th*/
      }
    }
  }
  tbody{
    /*style for tbody*/
    tr{
      &.even{
        /*style for tr.even*/
      }
      &.odd{
        /*style for tr.odd*/
```

```
        }
      }
    }
  }
```

## Variable

This feature is useful when some css property value FREQUENCY is higher. It means some value used repeatedly. There are many scenarios in development where we want to match the color of different HTML element. In this scenario SASS provides the global variable which can be used across the css file. Below code is a simple example (.SCSS) of variable declaration and its call in different places.

```
/* SASS variable declaration Example, $textcolor is a sass variable holds the value
'red'*/
$textcolor:red;
table{
  /*style for table level*/
  thead{
    /*style for thead*/
    tr{
      /*style for tr*/
      th{
        /*SASS variable call example, $textcolor is called which has value 'red used
for background*/
        background:$textcolor;
      }
    }
  }
  tbody{
    /*style for tbody*/
    tr{
      &.even{
        /*SASS variable call example, $textcolor is called which has value 'red used
for font color*/
        color:$textcolor;
      }
      &.odd{
        /*style for tr.odd*/
      }
```

```
        }
      }
    }
```

## Mixin

This feature is helpful for the scenarios where you need to do some process based on CONDITION dynamically. It is similar to a function where we do some process and return different response based on response. For Example, There are many situations where we need different font styling for different parts of web application like header, content, footer, sidebar and content title. A MIXIN is declared using **@mixin** annotation. A MIXIN can be used by calling it through **@include** annotation. Bellow code is simple example (SCSS) file showing MIXIN declaration and its call in two different places.

```
/*MIXIN: declaration font styling*/
@mixin myappFont($fontfamily,$fontsize,$fontcolor,$fontweight) {
 font-family: left;
 font-size:$fontsize;
 color:$fontcolor;
 font-weight:$fontweight;
}
thead th{
   /*Calling the MIXIN myappFont*/
   @include myappFont(georgia,10px,red,400);
}
tbody td{
   /*Calling the MIXIN myappFont*/
   @include myappFont(arial,12px,blue,600);
}
```

## Inheritance

This feature provides the inheritance capability to a css developer. It helps in DERIVING style properties from different css classes. In some scenarios while writing CSS styles we need to incorporate different style from multiple classes. In this situation SASS selector inheritance is more useful. To inherit from a css class **@extend** annotation is used. Below code shows a simple example how a class is inheriting/extending to/from another css class.

```
/*A CSS class selector*/
.my-font{
  font-family:georgia;
```

```scss
    font-size:10px
  }
  /*INHERITANCE: deriving css properties from another class*/
  .your-font {
   @extend .my-font;
   color: red;
  }
```

Finally the below SCSS code shows all the SASS feature use to style our student list HTML markup,

```scss
  /*VARIABLE DECLARATION: common css property values are declared as    global
  to use in multiple places and maintains similarity in styling
  */
  $headerBackground: #000;
  $yellowBackground: #FFCC00;
  $greyBackground: #808080;
  /*MIXIN DECLARATION: A mixin is similar to a function
   * which return a set of
   * css property configured dynamically
   */
  @mixin myFont($fontFamily, $fontSize, $fontColor) {
   font-family: $fontFamily;
   font-size: $fontSize;
   color: $fontColor;
  }
  table.ts-student-table {
   .headertext {
    font-weight: bold;
   }
   thead {
    /*VARIBLE CALL: replaces the value of the variable*/
    background: $headerBackground;
    color: #fff;
    /*INHERITANCE: derives the style from headertext class*/
    @extend headertext;
   }
   tbody {
    tr.even {
```

```
    /*MIXIN CALL: calling a mixin is similar to calling a function*/
    @include myFont(Georgia, 10px, #0000ff);
    background: $yellowBackground;

  }
  tr.odd {
    @include myFont(arial, 10px, #ff0000);
    background: $greyBackground;

  }
 }
}
```

The above SCSS file get converted to corresponding CSS file .The below CSS code shows the output/CSS version of the above code.

```
/*myFont: is a mixin, similar to a function
Which return a set of
Css property configured dynamically*/
/* line 14, ../sass/my-style.scss */
table.ts-student-table .headertext {
  font-weight: bold;
}
/* line 17, ../sass/my-style.scss */
table.ts-student-table thead {
  background: black;
  color: #fff;
}
/* line 24, ../sass/my-style.scss */
table.ts-student-table tbody tr.even {
  font-family: Georgia;
  font-size: 10px;
  color: blue;
  background: #ffcc00;
}
/* line 28, ../sass/my-style.scss */
table.ts-student-table tbody tr.odd {
  font-family: arial;
  font-size: 10px;
  color: red;
  background: gray;
```

}

Below code shows the converted css file with HTML markup and its result,

```
/*myFont: is a mixin, similar to a function
which return a set of
css property configured dynamically*/
/* line 14, ../sass/my-style.scss */
table.ts-student-table .headertext {
  font-weight: bold;
}
/* line 17, ../sass/my-style.scss */
table.ts-student-table thead {
  background: black;
  color: #fff;
}
/* line 24, ../sass/my-style.scss */
table.ts-student-table tbody tr.even {
  font-family: Georgia;
  font-size: 10px;
  color: blue;
  background: #ffcc00;
}
/* line 28, ../sass/my-style.scss */
table.ts-student-table tbody tr.odd {
  font-family: arial;
  font-size: 10px;
  color: red;
  background: gray;
}
```

The output will look like below screenshot,

| NAME | ROLL | MARK | COUNTRY |
|------|------|------|---------|
| Sandeep | 001 | 235 | India |
| John | 002 | 335 | US |
| Stephen | 003 | 135 | UK |
| Philip | 004 | 139 | Germany |
| Sandeep | 001 | 235 | India |
| John | 002 | 335 | US |
| Stephen | 003 | 135 | UK |
| Philip | 004 | 139 | Germany |
| Sandeep | 001 | 235 | India |
| John | 002 | 335 | US |
| Stephen | 003 | 135 | UK |
| Philip | 004 | 139 | Germany |

# Chapter 4 Control Statement in SASS

SASS provides control statement to better css authoring. Some of the useful controls are @IF, @IF..ELSE, @FOR, @WHILE, @EACH.

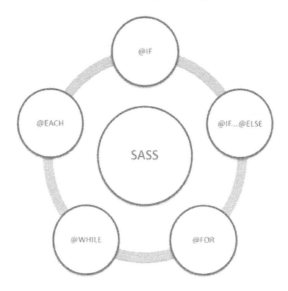

## Objective

In this Demo, "We will see how to use IF, FOR, WHILE and EACH statement while writing SCSS code".

## Going Ahead

Below HTML markup is been used for styling with css classes. This markup has two container DIV elements where we are going to apply our SCSS generated css classes.

```
<!DOCTYPE html>
<html>
<head>
  <title>More on SASS</title>
  <link rel="stylesheet" type="text/css" href="my-style.css">
</head>
<body>
 <div class='container-1'>
```

```
    container-1
  </div>
  <div class='container-2'>
    container-2
  </div>
  </body>
  </html>
```

Below SCSS file shows the code for styling this markup and detail explanation of each block.

```scss
/*Global values*/
$containerHeight : 50px;
$containerWidth : 600px;
$backgroundColor:#000000;
$fontSize:16px;
/*This is parent container from which all other container classes are extended*/
.container{
  height: $containerHeight;
  width :  $containerWidth;
  background: $backgroundColor;
  margin: 10px;
}
/*fontColor: This is a SCSS MIXIN function which takes a string as input and checks
 *its name.If it is container 1 then it makes the font color as #FF0000
 *else it makes the font color as #0000FF
 */
@mixin fontColor($containername){
  @if $containername == container-2 {
   color:#FF0000;
  }
  @else{
   color:#0000FF;
  }
}
/*This is container-1 it is extending container class and
 *Calling the fontColor MIXIN by passing it class string.This results
 *in font color #0000FF
 */
```

```scss
.container-1{
  @extend .container;
  @include fontColor(container-1);
}
/*This is container-2 it is extending container class and
*Calling the fontColor MIXIN by passing it class string.This results
*in font color #FF0000
*/
.container-2{
  @extend .container;
  @include fontColor(container-2);
}
/*FOR : This loop is for styling the border for both
 *the contaner-1 and container-2.For every iteration
 *of this loop it is multiplying the iteration number
 *with 5px.Hence container-1 will have 5px border and container-2
 *will have 10px border.
 */
@for $index from 1 through 2 {
  .container-#{$index} {
    border: 5px * $index solid  grey;
  }
}
/*EACH : This loop is for styling the font size for both
 *the contaner-1 and container-2.For every iteration
 *of this loop it is summing the previous font size with 10
 *.Hence container-1 will have 26px font size and container-2
 *will have 36px font size.
 */
@each $container in container-1,container-2 {
  $fontSize : $fontSize + 10;
  .#{$container} {
  font-size: $fontSize;
  }
}
/*WHILE : This loop is for styling the font weight for both
 *the contaner-1 and container-2.For every iteration
```

```
    *of this loop it is multiplying the container number with 300.
    *Hence container-1 will have 300 font weight and container-2
    *will have 600 font weight.
    */
   $totalContainer: 2;
   @while $totalContainer &gt; 0 {
     .container-#{$totalContainer} {
      font-weight:300 * $totalContainer;
     }
     $totalContainer: $totalContainer - 1;
   }
```
Below CSS file has the compiled SCSS code.

```
  /*Global values*/
  /*This is parent container from which all other container classes are extended*/
  .container, .container-1, .container-2 {
    height: 50px;
    width: 600px;
    background: black;
    margin: 10px; }
  /*fontColor: This is a SCSS MIXIN function which takes a string as input and checks
   *its name. If it is container 1 then it makes the font color as #FF0000
   *else it makes the font color as #0000FF
   */
  /*This is container-1 it is extending container class and
   *Calling the fontColor MIXIN by passing it class string. This results
   *in font color #0000FF
   */
  .container-1 {
    color: #0000FF; }
  /*This is container-2 it is extending container class and
   *Calling the fontColor MIXIN by passing it class string. This results
   *in font color #FF0000
   */
  .container-2 {
    color: #FF0000; }
  /*FOR : This loop is for styling the border for both
   *the contaner-1 and container-2.For every iteration
```

*of this loop it is multiplying the iteration number
*with 5px. Hence container-1 will have 5px border and container-2
*will have 10px border.
*/
.container-1 {
  border: 5px solid grey; }
.container-2 {
  border: 10px solid grey; }
/*EACH : This loop is for styling the font size for both
 *the contaner-1 and container-2.For every iteration
 *of this loop it is summing the previous font size with 10
 *.Hence container-1 will have 26px font size and container-2
 *will have 36px font size.
 */
.container-1 {
  font-size: 26px; }
.container-2 {
  font-size: 36px; }


/*WHILE : This loop is for styling the font weight for both
 *the contaner-1 and container-2.For every iteration
 *of this loop it is multiplying the container number with 300.
 *Hence container-1 will have 300 font weight and container-2
 *will have 600 font weight.
 */
.container-2 {
  font-weight: 600; }
.container-1 {
  font-weight: 300; }


The below screenshot shows the output of the above markup in browser.

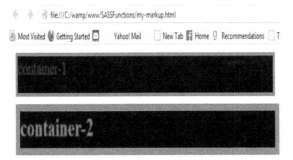

# Chapter 5 SASS Colour Methods

SASS provide bunch of inbuilt methods to make the CSS Authoring Simple and easy. RGB/RGBA (Red, Green, and Blue with or without Alpha) and HSL/HSLA (Hue, Saturation, and Lightness with or without Alpha) is popular used color model for web development. RGB model is known to everybody.

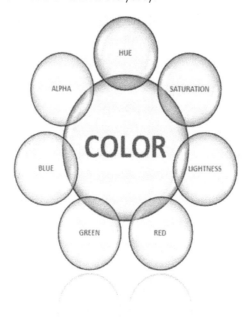

## Objective

In this Demo, "We will explore SASS inbuilt methods for COLORING".

## Going Ahead

In this model all colors are formed by combination of three colors i.e., red, green and blue. HSL model is new for web development. In this model a color is made by hue, saturation and lightness.

- HUE : is the pure color without tint or shade.
- SATURATION: is the spread of a color.
- LIGHTNESS: is the intensity of a color.

In this chapter we have used inbuilt color methods from SASS to set the background of DIV elements. Below HTML markup is used for the applying css classes.

```html
<!DOCTYPE html>
<html>
<head>
  <title>SASS Color Methods</title>
  <link rel="stylesheet" type="text/css" href="my-style.css">
</head>
<body>
<h4>HSL Color Methods: </h4>
    <div class='container-one'>
      background: $backgroundColor;
    </div>
    <div class='container-two'>
      background: darken($backgroundColor, 30%);
    </div>
    <div class='container-three'>
      background: lighten($backgroundColor, 30%);
    </div>
    <div class='container-four'>
      background: invert($backgroundColor);
    </div>
    <div class='container-five'>
      background: complement($backgroundColor);
    </div>
    <div class='container-six'>
      background: saturate($backgroundColor,90%);
    </div>
    <div class='container-seven'>
      background: desaturate($backgroundColor,90%);
    </div>
    <div class='container-eight'>
      background: adjust-hue($backgroundColor,90%);
    </div>
    <div class='container-nine'>
      background: saturation($backgroundColor);
    </div>
```

```
    <div class='container-ten'>
      background: hue($backgroundColor);
    </div>
    <div class='container-eleven'>
      background: hsl(180, 20, 30);
    </div>
    <div class='container-tweleve'>
      background: hsla(10, 20, 30,0.2);
    </div>
    <h4>RGB Color Methods: </h4>
    <div class='container-thirteen'>
      background: rgb($myredcolor, $mygreencolor, $mybluecolor);
    </div>
    <div class='container-fourteen'>
      background: rgba($myredcolor, $mygreencolor, $mybluecolor, 0.2);
    </div>
    <div class='container-fifteen'>
      background: red($backgroundColor);
    </div>
    <div class='container-sixteen'>
      background: green($backgroundColor);
    </div>
    <div class='container-seventeen'>
      background: blue($backgroundColor);
    </div>
    <div class='container-eighteen'>
      background: mix(rgb($myredcolor, $mygreencolor, $mybluecolor), #808080);
    </div>
  </body>
</html>
```

This SCSS file contains the SASS code for coloring different DIV elements. Each container is assigned with a css class .Each css class has different SASS coloring method for applying to its background.

```
$containerHeight : 20px;
$containerWidth : 600px;
$backgroundColor:#00FF00;
$fontColor:#FF0000;
```

```scss
/*HSL colors -- tutorialsavvy.com*/
.container{
 height: $containerHeight;
 width :  $containerWidth;
 color:$fontColor;
 border:1px solid #CoCoCo;
 text-align:left;
}
.container-one{
 @extend .container;
 background: $backgroundColor;


}
.container-two{
 @extend .container;
 background: darken($backgroundColor, 30%);
}
.container-three{
 @extend .container;
 background: lighten($backgroundColor, 30%);
}
.container-four{
 @extend .container;
 background: invert($backgroundColor);
}
.container-five{
 @extend .container;
 background: complement($backgroundColor);
}
.container-six{
 @extend .container;
 background: saturate($backgroundColor,90%);
}
.container-seven{
 @extend .container;
 background: desaturate($backgroundColor,90%);
}
```

```scss
.container-seven{
 @extend .container;
 background: desaturate($backgroundColor,90%);
}
.container-eight{
 @extend .container;
 background: adjust-hue($backgroundColor,90%);
}
.container-nine{
 @extend .container;
 background: saturation($backgroundColor);
}
.container-ten{
 @extend .container;
 background: hue($backgroundColor);
}

.container-eleven{
 @extend .container;
 background: hsl(180, 20, 30);
}

.container-tweleve{
 @extend .container;
 background: hsla(10, 20, 30,0.2);
}

/*RGB colors -- tutorialsavvy.com*/
$myredcolor : 35;
$mygreencolor : 95;
$mybluecolor : 105;
.container-thirteen{
 @extend .container;
 background: rgb($myredcolor, $mygreencolor, $mybluecolor);
}
.container-fourteen{
 @extend .container;
```

```
    background: rgba($myredcolor, $mygreencolor, $mybluecolor, 0.2);
   }
  .container-fifteen{
   @extend .container;
   background: red($backgroundColor);
   }
  .container-sixteen{
   @extend .container;
   background: green($backgroundColor);
   }
  .container-seventeen{
   @extend .container;
   background: blue($backgroundColor);
   }
  .container-eighteen {
   @extend .container;
   background: mix(rgb($myredcolor, $mygreencolor, $mybluecolor), #808080);
   }
```

This is the generated CSS file from the above SCSS file. You can compare both the file and can find the equivalent css value for each SASS coloring methods.

```
/*HSL colors -- tutorialsavvy.com*/
.container, .container-one, .container-two, .container-three, .container-four,
.container-five, .container-six, .container-seven, .container-eight, .container-nine,
.container-ten, .container-eleven, .container-tweleve, .container-thirteen, .container-
fourteen, .container-fifteen, .container-sixteen, .container-seventeen, .container-
eighteen {
 height: 20px;
 width: 600px;
 color: red;
 border: 1px solid #CoCoCo;
 text-align: left; }

.container-one {
 background: lime; }

.container-two {
 background: #006600; }

.container-three {
```

```css
  background: #99ff99; }

.container-four {
  background: magenta; }

.container-five {
  background: magenta; }

.container-six {
  background: lime; }

.container-seven {
  background: #738c73; }

.container-seven {
  background: #738c73; }

.container-eight {
  background: #007fff; }

.container-nine {
  background: 100%; }

.container-ten {
  background: 120deg; }

.container-eleven {
  background: #3d5c5c; }

.container-tweleve {
  background: rgba(92, 66, 61, 0.2); }

/*RGB colors -- tutorialsavvy.com*/
.container-thirteen {
  background: #235f69; }

.container-fourteen {
  background: rgba(35, 95, 105, 0.2); }

.container-fifteen {
  background: 0; }

.container-sixteen {
  background: 255; }
```

```
.container-seventeen {
 background: 0; }

.container-eighteen {
 background: #516f74; }
```

The output of the code will look like below screenshot.

**HSL Color Methods:-**

background: $backgroundColor;
background: lighten($backgroundColor, 30%);

background: saturate($backgroundColor, 90%);
background: desaturate($backgroundColor, 90%);
background: adjust-hue($backgroundColor, 90%);
background: saturation($backgroundColor);
background: hue($backgroundColor);

background: hsla(10, 20, 30,0.2);

**RGB Color Methods:-**

background: rgba($myredcolor, $mygreencolor, $mybluecolor, 0.2);
background: red($backgroundColor);
background: green($backgroundColor);
background: blue($backgroundColor);

# Chapter 6 SASS Output Format

SASS provides 4 different types of output formats for compiled css. These output formats can be configured according to debugging requirements.

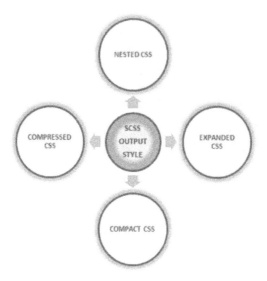

Objective

In this Demo, "We will explore 4 different output formats with example".

Going Ahead

All these formats are explained below.

Nested

- This format is based on the relationship among the css classes.
- This is better for understanding css classes' relation.
- It is useful for maintaining large css files.

Expanded

- This format maintains all spacing among css classes with curly braces ending in a new line.
- It is better for development purpose.
- It is human readable format.

Compact

- It takes less space than nested and expanded format.
- It gives emphasis on css selectors.
- All the style properties are defined in a single line per selector.

Compressed

- It takes very less space.
- All css selector including style properties defined in single line.
- Better for production purpose

We have used new-style.scss file for this demo. This file contains some scss code about a HTML DIV element. The below code shows the content of this scss file.

```
/*tutorialsavvy: SCSS file*/
$containerHeight : 50px;
$containerWidth : 600px;
$backgroundColor:#000000;
$fontSize:16px;
/*This is parent container from which all other container classes are extended*/
.container{
 height: $containerHeight;
 width : $containerWidth;
 background: $backgroundColor;
 margin: 10px;
 font-size: $fontSize;
}
.container-one{
 @extend .container;
 padding:2px;
}
```

Let's apply the nested output format using '--style' switch with SASS watch option and the output file will be new-style-nested.css.

sass --watch --style 'nested' new-style.scss:new-style-nested.css

The output will look like below css code.

```
/*tutorialsavvy: SCSS file*/
/*This is parent container from which all other container classes are extended*/
.container, .container-one {
  height: 50px;
  width: 600px;
  background: black;
  margin: 10px;
  font-size: 16px; }
.container-one {
  padding: 2px; }
```

Let's apply the expanded output format using '--style' switch with SASS watch option and the output file will be new-style-expanded.css.

sass --watch --style 'expanded' new-style.scss:new-style-expanded.css

The output will look like below css code.

```
/*tutorialsavvy: SCSS file*/
/*This is parent container from which all other container classes are extended*/
.container, .container-one {
  height: 50px;
```

```
    width: 600px;
    background: black;
    margin: 10px;
    font-size: 16px;
}
.container-one {
    padding: 2px;
}
```

Let's apply the compact output format using '--style' switch with SASS watch option and the output file will be new-style-compact.css.

sass --watch --style 'compact' new-style.scss:new-style-compact.css

The output will look like below css code.

```
/*tutorialsavvy: SCSS file*/
/*This is parent container from which all other container classes are extended*/
.container, .container-one { height: 50px; width: 600px; background: black; margin: 10px; font-size: 16px; }
.container-one { padding: 2px; }
```

Let's apply the compressed output format using '--style' switch with SASS watch option and the output file will be new-style-compressed.css.

```
sass --watch --style 'compressed' new-style.scss:new-style-compressed.css
```

The output will look like below css code.

```
.container,
.container-one{height:50px;width:600px;background:#000;margin:10px;font-size:16px}
.container-one{padding:2px}
```

# Chapter 7 Compass Watcher

Compass is another CSS authoring framework based on SASS. It also has some additional modules like blueprint for advanced CSS authoring. However In this chapter we will only learn about compass watcher. You can find more information about Compass in http://compass-style.org .

### Objective

In this Chapter, "We will learn to install and configure compass watcher for CSS authoring".

### Going Ahead

Compass can be installed as ruby gem. Use gem install compass command to install compass. Below screenshot shows the installation of compass.

```
            C:\windows\system32\cmd.exe - gem install compass

C:\Windows\system32>gem install compass
Successfully installed sass-3.2.14
Successfully installed compass-0.12.3
2 gems installed
Installing ri documentation for sass-3.2.14...
```

Compass can be initialized using compass **init** command on the project. Below screenshot shows the initialization of compass for **MyTestProject**.

```
C:\windows\system32\cmd.exe                         –  □   ✕

E:\MyTestProject>compass init
directory sass/
directory stylesheets/
    create config.rb
    create sass/screen.scss
    create sass/print.scss
    create sass/ie.scss
    create stylesheets/ie.css
    create stylesheets/print.css
    create stylesheets/screen.css

*****************************************************************
Congratulations! Your compass project has been created.

You may now add and edit sass stylesheets in the sass subdirectory of your project.

Sass files beginning with an underscore are called partials and won't be
compiled to CSS, but they can be imported into other sass stylesheets.

You can configure your project by editing the config.rb configuration file.

You must compile your sass stylesheets into CSS when they change.
This can be done in one of the following ways:
 1. To compile on demand:
    compass compile [path/to/project]
 2. To monitor your project for changes and automatically recompile:
    compass watch [path/to/project]

More Resources:
 * Website: http://compass-style.org/
 * Sass: http://sass-lang.com
 * Community: http://groups.google.com/group/compass-users/
```

The Project will look like below screenshot. It has created Sass and stylesheet folder in the path.

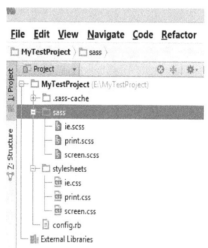

Config.rb file contains all the settings for the compass configuration.

```
# Require any additional compass plugins here.
# Set this to the root of your project when deployed:
http_path = "/"
css_dir = "stylesheets"
```

```
sass_dir = "sass"
images_dir = "images"
javascripts_dir = "javascripts"
```

Details of the config.rb file are below:-

- All the SCSS files are present in sass folder. The sass_dir contains the reference to this directory.

- The stylesheet folder contains the entire converted CSS file. css_dir contains reference to the stylesheets folder.

# Chapter 8 BootStrap3 SCSS Build

Bootstrap source code is also available in SASS format.The use of SASS format of Bootstrap is really useful for theme creation.We can modify each SCSS file of bootstrap and generate our own CSS file.

You can also use Bower tool to download Bootstrap source files in SCSS format.Below screenshot shows Bower installing Bootstrap SASSPackage.

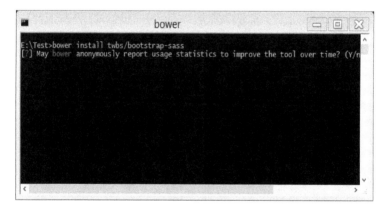

Now you can check bower_component folder created inside it.Compass watcher can be started using compass watch command. The watcher read all its configuration form config file and checks for any change in SCSS files and updates the corresponding stylesheet inside the folder.

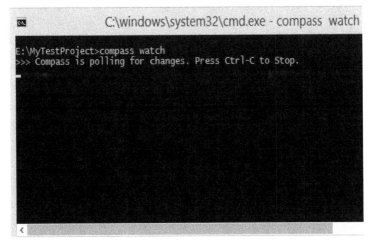

Now if you check inside the folder you will find css, fonts and js directory present. We can copy these folders to our project and configure compass watcher to track any changes.

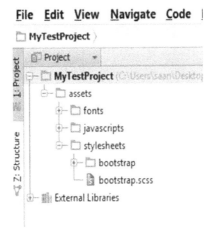

You can see all the SCSS file related to Bootstrap in the bootstrap folder. Below screenshot shows all the Bootstrap module.

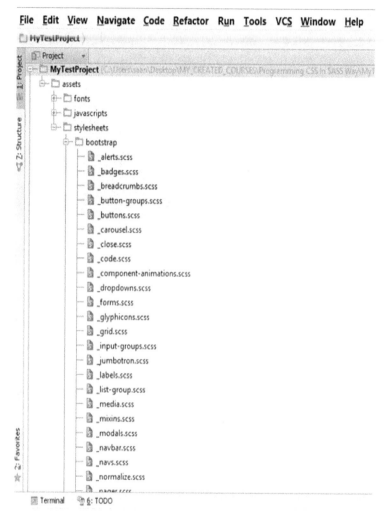

To initialize compass issue compass init method. This will generate a config.rb file.

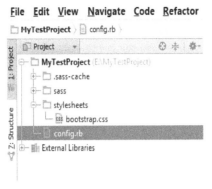

The compass watcher can be started using compass watch command .Below screenshot shows watcher in action in command prompt.

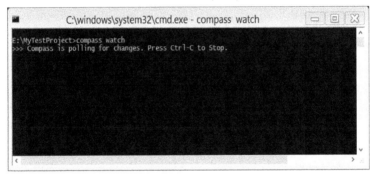

If you notice some SCSS files are prefixed Underscore ( _ ) files. These means these modules are not the main module and will be combined in the single Bootstrap SCSS file. The main bootstrap.scss file has imported all the other sub scss file in it. Below bootstrap.scss file contains the below code.

```
// Core variables and mixins
@import "variables";
@import "mixins";
// Reset
@import "normalize";
@import "print";
// Core CSS
@import "scaffolding";
@import "type";
@import "code";
@import "grid";
@import "tables";
@import "forms";
```

```scss
@import "buttons";
// Components
@import "component-animations";
@import "glyphicons";
@import "dropdowns";
@import "button-groups";
@import "input-groups";
@import "navs";
@import "navbar";
@import "breadcrumbs";
@import "pagination";
@import "pager";
@import "labels";
@import "badges";
@import "jumbotron";
@import "thumbnails";
@import "alerts";
@import "progress-bars";
@import "media";
@import "list-group";
@import "panels";
@import "wells";
@import "close";
// Components w/ JavaScript
@import "modals";
@import "tooltip";
@import "popovers";
@import "carousel";
// Utility classes
@import "utilities";
@import "responsive-utilities";
```

Let's do some changes in the **_button.scss** file .Check the below screenshot compass watcher has detected the changes in the **_button.scss** file and it is migrating those changes to bootstrap.css file.

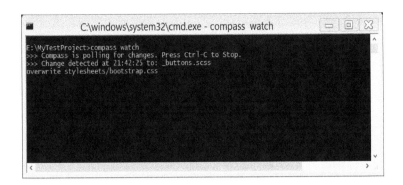

# Chapter 9 SCSS Example

Example 1: Creating Menubar

In this example we will create a menu bar using SCSS file. The menu bar is a unordered list container and Each menu item is an LI element containing an anchor link.The HTML markup code for menu bar is present in menubar.html file.

```html
<!DOCTYPE html>
<html>
<head>
  <link rel="stylesheet" href="stylesheets/menu-recipe.css">
</head>
<body>
<ul class="ts-menu-container">
  <li><a href="#">Home</a></li>
  <li><a href="#">About</a></li>
  <li><a href="#">Produt</a></li>
  <li><a href="#">Contact</a></li>
</ul>
</body>
</html>
```

The SCSS file menu-recipe.scss has all the scss code for creating menu bar.

```scss
.ts-menu-container{
  background: rgba(0,0,0,0.5);
  padding: 15px;
  border-radius: 10%;
  border-radius: 5px;
  width:60%;
  li{
    display: inline-block;
    font-family: monospace;
    font-size: 20px;
    margin-left: 10%;
```

```scss
    padding: 10px 20px;
    cursor: pointer;
    transition:all 1s ease;
    border-radius: 50%;
     a{
      text-decoration: none;
      color: #FFFFFF;
     }
     &:hover{
      background: rgba(0,0,0,1);
     }
    }
}
```

Compass watcher has generated the corresponding CSS code in `menu-resipe.css` file.

```css
/* line 1, ../sass/menu-recipe.scss */
.ts-menu-container {
  background: rgba(0, 0, 0, 0.5);
  padding: 15px;
  border-radius: 10%;
  border-radius: 5px;
}
/* line 6, ../sass/menu-recipe.scss */
.ts-menu-container li {
  display: inline-block;
  font-family: monospace;
  font-size: 20px;
  margin-left: 15%;
  padding: 10px 20px;
  cursor: pointer;
  transition: all 1s ease;
  border-radius: 50%;
}
/* line 16, ../sass/menu-recipe.scss */
.ts-menu-container li a {
  text-decoration: none;
  color: #FFFFFF;
}
```

```scss
/* line 20, ../sass/menu-recipe.scss */
ts-menu-container li:hover {
  background: black;
}
```

The menu will look like below screenshot.

On Hover of each menu item the transition will take place and it will look like below screenshot.

Example 2: Nth Child Selection

In this Example we will learn how to use nth child css property. We have 9 child div elements inside the **ts-parent** element. In this example we are increasing the width of each child by Nth *100px.It means the children will have 100px, 200px, 300px...and 900px width.

```html
<!DOCTYPE html>
<html>
<head>
  <link rel="stylesheet" href="stylesheets/nthchild-recipe.css">
</head>
<body>
<div class="ts-parent">
  <div class="item">1</div>
  <div class="item">2</div>
  <div class="item">3</div>
  <div class="item">4</div>
  <div class="item">5</div>
  <div class="item">6</div>
  <div class="item">7</div>
```

```
   <div class="item">8</div>
   <div class="item">9</div>
</div>
</body>
</html>
```

The SCSS file below contains the code for accomplishing the above idea. For this we have followed below steps:-

- Mixin myNumber which takes an input width applies to the width property.
- A SASS script For loop is iterated form 1 to 9 and passed as argument to Mixin myNumber.#{} is act as holder for value .

```
@mixin myNumber($no) {
  width:$no;
}
.ts-parent{
  @for $index from 1 through 9{
   div.item:nth-child(#{$index}){
    @include myNumber(#{$index * 100px});
    font-size:20px;
    background: #000;
    color:#fff;
    margin:2px;
   }
  }
}
```

Generated CSS file for the above SCSS code is as below. The css file has all the 9 child element style separately.

```
/* line 11, ../sass/nthchild-recipe.scss */
.ts-parent div.item:nth-child(1) {
  width: 100px;
  font-size: 20px;
  background: #000;
  color: #fff;
  margin: 2px;
}
/* line 11, ../sass/nthchild-recipe.scss */
.ts-parent div.item:nth-child(2) {
```

```
  width: 200px;
  font-size: 20px;
  background: #000;
  color: #fff;
  margin: 2px;
}
/* line 11, ../sass/nthchild-recipe.scss */
.ts-parent div.item:nth-child(3) {
  width: 300px;
  font-size: 20px;
  background: #000;
  color: #fff;
  margin: 2px;
}
/* line 11, ../sass/nthchild-recipe.scss */
.ts-parent div.item:nth-child(4) {
  width: 400px;
  font-size: 20px;
  background: #000;
  color: #fff;
  margin: 2px;
}
/* line 11, ../sass/nthchild-recipe.scss */
.ts-parent div.item:nth-child(5) {
  width: 500px;
  font-size: 20px;
  background: #000;
  color: #fff;
  margin: 2px;
}
/* line 11, ../sass/nthchild-recipe.scss */
.ts-parent div.item:nth-child(6) {
  width: 600px;
  font-size: 20px;
  background: #000;
  color: #fff;
  margin: 2px;
```

```
}
/* line 11, ../sass/nthchild-recipe.scss */
.ts-parent div.item:nth-child(7) {
 width: 700px;
 font-size: 20px;
 background: #000;
 color: #fff;
 margin: 2px;
}
/* line 11, ../sass/nthchild-recipe.scss */
.ts-parent div.item:nth-child(8) {
 width: 800px;
 font-size: 20px;
 background: #000;
 color: #fff;
 margin: 2px;
}
/* line 11, ../sass/nthchild-recipe.scss */
.ts-parent div.item:nth-child(9) {
 width: 900px;
 font-size: 20px;
 background: #000;
 color: #fff;
 margin: 2px;
}
```

Output will look like below,

# Chapter 10 Debuqqinq With Chrome

Chrome provides an awesome developer console to debug front end code. In this chapter we will see how this debugger is helping us to debug a SCSS file.

CHROME BROWSER

Let's inspect recipe 1 in chrome browser. The menu bar has background in rgba(0,0,0,0.5).

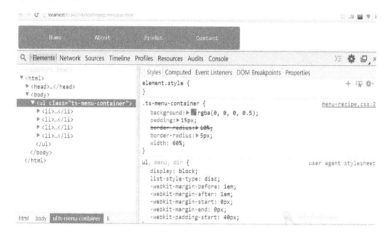

Let's change the background color. If you click on the menu-recipe.css line 2 noted in Chrome developer toolbar. It will show you the referred the SCSS file.

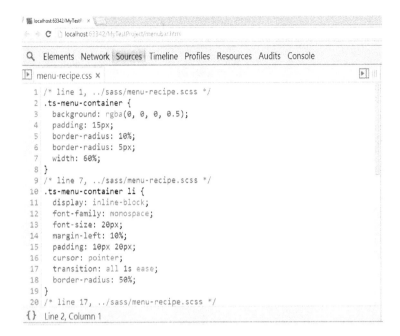

You can find the exact SCSS file name with correct Line number that refers to the background color. Now you can go that location and change the color at that position.

# About The Author

Sandeep Kumar Patel is a senior web developer and founder of www.tutorialsavvy.com, a widely read programming blog since 2012. He has more than four years of experience in object-oriented JavaScript and JSON-based web applications development. He is GATE-2005 Information Technology (IT) qualified and has a Master's degree from VIT University, Vellore.

 You can know more about him from his

-LinkedIn profile (http://www.linkedin.com/in/techblogger).

-He has received the Dzone Most Valuable Blogger (MVB) award for technical publications related to web technologies. His article can be viewed at http://www.dzone.com/users/sandeepgiet.

-He has also received the Java Code Geek (JCG) badge for a technical article published in JCG. His article can be viewed at http://www.javacodegeeks.com/author/sandeep-kumar-patel/.

-Author of "Instant GSON" for Packt publication, http://www.packtpub.com/create-json-data-java-objects-implement-with-gson-library/book
Questions or comments? E-mail me at sandeeppateltech@gmail.com or find me on the following social networks:-

-Facebook Page: http://www.facebook.com/SandeepTechTutorials .
-Tutorial Blog: http://www.tutorialsavvy.com

# One Last Thing...

When you turn the page, Kindle will give you the opportunity to rate this book and share your thoughts on Facebook and Twitter. If you believe the book is worth sharing, please would you take a few seconds to let your friends know about it? If it turns out to make a difference in their professional lives, they'll be forever grateful to you, as will I.

All the best,
Sandeep Kumar Patel.

www.ingramcontent.com/pod-product-compliance
Lightning Source LLC
LaVergne TN
LVHW052315060326
832902LV00021B/3907